SECRETS TO TEAM DEVELOPMENT

Best Practices For Building A Strong, Effective Team

CHARLES S. BRETON

Table Of Contents:

INTRODUCTION:

Teams are not a novel concept. The majority of us have some experience playing on teams. It might have been a work team, a sports team, a debate team, a group formed to address a challenge, a nonprofit group, or a group assembled to tackle a problem. We shall each read the pages that follow with a perspective influenced by our history due to our unique experiences. Although most of us have had team experiences that were far from ideal—the majority of us have never been a part of a truly high-performance team—I want to encourage you to put those experiences behind you. You might be on the cusp of a huge innovation if you can approach the concept or teams with fresh eyes. You might experience a breakthrough in your quality of life, a breakthrough in performance, a breakthrough in the growth of others, and a breakthrough in your leadership potential.

Here is a little narrative. The strength of the ideas given here and my faith in the enormous untapped potential of your team, rather than the strength of the story, are the foundations of this pledge. Delivering extraordinary, long-lasting results is harder than talking about getting people to cooperate. It is difficult and messy to pursue high-performance teams as a performance improvement strategy. But this is only one of the factors that make the concept itself such an alluring strategy for gaining a competitive advantage. Another is the magnitude of the challenge.

Teams frequently require a team leader. The driving factor that unites the team members is the team leader. The team leader's job is somewhat crucial since he or she serves as the glue that holds the members of the group together. At the same time, the team leader establishes and stresses the team's aims and ideals.

This book is full of straightforward concepts that, with the right leadership, may completely transform your team's effectiveness. What you choose to do after finishing this book will be up to you.NI've provided some suggested action items and a High-Performance Team Assessment to aid you in finding the solution to that query. As you plot your course, I sincerely hope you will find these tools useful.

Prepare for an incredible trip as you get set to expand your leadership, and your team, and produce spectacular outcomes!

CHAPTER ONE

TEAM
DEVELOPMENT/MANAGEMENT

Via a variety of activities, team development is a management approach used to increase the effectiveness and performance of workgroups. Forming an effective team requires a lot of skills, analysis, and observation. The organization's mission and objectives are the only motivation in this situation.
You're probably asking now, "How to Create a Fantastic Team?"

A great team takes a lot of abilities and mental fortitude to form. Typically, firms employ managers based on their specialization in team-building abilities. The ties between group members get stronger as a result of team development. Each member respects one another's differences as well as their own, and they all work for the same objectives. The daily interaction that staff members have while collaborating to complete their responsibilities might be included in team development. If the group takes an effort to build a set of team rules, it will help this type of natural team development. Members of the group benefit from knowing how to behave both within the team and with the rest of the organization thanks to these norms. Structured exercises and activities led by team members can also be a part of team development. Alternatively, managers can hire an outside person to facilitate meetings if they have the right goals and funding. An expert outside facilitator can help your team improve more quickly. The manager in charge of team development must be able to identify the team member's strengths and limitations and put together the ideal group of individuals with a variety of skill sets. He needs to concentrate on building trust and good interpersonal relationships among the team members. Using a variety of team-building exercises, the manager must promote engagement and communication among the team members as well as help them cope with stress. He needs to explain to the team members what the organization's goals and objectives are. To guide the team toward achieving the organizational goals, he must also clearly define each member's job.

Other initiatives are taken to encourage team members and improve the group's performance, including team development. Simply said, you can't count on your team to perform well on its own. A driving force is necessary. Team building exercises involve a variety of tasks completed to grow a team member, inspire him, and get the greatest performance out of him. Being human means that we all value praise. Any person who does particularly well deserves to be favorably received in public. He's content and inspired to do even better the following time. If a team member has an original idea, give him whatever will make him pleased. Never belittle or demoralize a teammate who hasn't performed well. Invite him to "Buckle Up"

Teams are a crucial component of productivity because many tasks require more than one person to complete them. To keep running, businesses rely on teams and efficient team leadership. Pitfalls like poor communication or a team member's lack of effort can thwart a team's success. Checkpoints are incorporated by team management to ensure successful team formation. It also supports sustaining a positive working environment and momentum throughout the team's existence till the objective is attained.

STAGES OF TEAM DEVELOPMENT

The dedication of a team to reflection and ongoing evaluation improves team effectiveness. Teams need to understand their team development to perform at a high level, in addition to measuring success in terms of achieving particular goals. The term "the terrible twos" refers to a period of early childhood that most people are familiar with; being aware of this developmental stage makes it easier to tolerate the nonstop stream of "No No No No No" that we would hear from a two-year-old. Teams go through development stages. In the middle of the 1960s, Bruce W. Tuckman created the framework that is most frequently used to describe the stages of development of a team. Although many authors have added to and modified Tuckman's ideas, his descriptions of Forming, Storming, Norming, and Performing offer a helpful framework for analyzing your team.

Understanding why things are happening on your team in certain ways can be a key step in the self-evaluation process. Each level of team development has its distinct recognizable sensations and behaviors. The four stages provide a valuable framework for identifying a team's behavioral patterns; they operate best as a springboard for team discussion as opposed to placing the team into a predetermined "diagnostic." However, team development is not necessarily a linear process, just as human development is not always linear (see the five-year-old who resumes thumb-sucking after the birth of a new sister). The team can optimize its procedure and productivity by having the means to recognize and comprehend the reasons behind modifications in team behaviors.

STAGE 1: FORMING

Feelings

Team members are typically thrilled to be a part of the team and eager about the work that lies ahead at the Forming stage of team growth. Members frequently have very high standards for their team experiences. They might also experience some anxiety as they consider how they will fit into the team and how their performance will fare.

Behaviors

Many queries from team members may be seen during the Forming stage, expressing both their excitement for the new team and any ambiguity or fear they may be experiencing regarding their position on the team.

Team Tasks

At the Forming stage, the team's main task is to establish a team with a clear structure, goals, direction, and duties so that members may start to develop trust. The team's mission and goals can be helped by a strong orientation or kick-off process, which can also serve to set expectations for the team's output and, more crucially, its workflow. Task completion may be below average during the Forming stage since the team's energy is largely directed toward identifying the team.

STAGE 2: STORMING

Feelings
Members learn that the team can't fulfill all of their early excitement and expectations as they make progress toward their goals. Their attention may divert from the work at hand to feelings of annoyance or rage at the team's performance or procedure. Members could voice worries about falling short of the group's objectives. Members test the team's ability to deal with conflict and respond to disagreements during the storming stage.

Behaviors
Storming stage interactions could be less courteous than Forming stage interactions, with open expressions of anger or disagreement about objectives, expectations, roles, and duties. Members may become frustrated with limitations that hinder their personal or team advancement; this dissatisfaction may be directed at other team members, the leadership of the team, or the team's sponsor. Team members may argue or start to question the

group's initial mission or objectives during the storming stage.

Team Tasks
To complete team tasks during the Storming stage of development, the team must refocus on its objectives and may need to divide more challenging objectives into more manageable chunks. The team may need to build abilities for managing conflict and group dynamics in addition to task-related abilities. Team members may be able to move over the dissatisfaction or misunderstanding they feel during the Storming stage by redefining the group's objectives, roles, and responsibilities.

STAGE 3: NORMING

Feelings
The team members start to reconcile the gap they sensed between their expectations and the reality of the team's experience during the Norming stage of team development. Members should feel more at ease expressing their "true" thoughts and feelings if the team is effective in

creating more accommodating and inclusive standards and expectations. When they come to understand how the diversity of viewpoints and experiences strengthens the team and enhances the quality of its output, team members feel a growing acceptance of their fellow team members. It's possible and encouraged to offer constructive critique. Members might enjoy the improved group cohesion as they begin to feel like a part of a team.

Behaviors

Members may actively try to settle issues and maintain harmony in the group throughout the Norming stage of behavior. Team members may communicate more frequently and meaningfully, and they may be more inclined to share ideas and solicit assistance from one another. Members of the team refocus on the established team norms and procedures and shift their attention back to the job at hand. Teams may start to create their language, including inside jokes and nicknames.

Team Tasks

Members become more focused on the team's objectives and exhibit a rise in productivity throughout the Norming stage, both in their individual and group work. The team can decide that now is the right time to assess their working methods and productivity.

Stage 4: Performing

Feelings

Members are pleased with the team's development during the performing stage. They are aware of their own (and each other's) strengths and flaws and share insights regarding personal and group processes. Members identify with the team as "bigger than the sum of its parts" and take pride in the team's accomplishments. Members have faith in both their skills and those of their teammates.

Behaviors

Members of the team can stop or fix issues that could hinder their work or their progress. Both a "can do" attitude and offers of help from one another are evident. The team's duties may have changed over time as individuals took on other tasks and responsibilities as needed. The team's effectiveness is improved by recognizing and utilizing member differences.

Team Tasks

The team achieves its objectives significantly during the performing stage. Both the level of skill and the level of commitment to the team's mission is very high. Team members should seek to constantly improve team development while also broadening their knowledge and abilities. Team progress or process accomplishments are tracked and recognized.

Is the process complete after the "Performing" stage?

While being a part of a high-performing team can be a really rewarding and growth-promoting experience, team development does not end there. The team must continue to concentrate on both process and product, defining new objectives as necessary. A team may cycle back to an earlier stage as a result of changes, such as new or departing members or significant alterations to the external environment. Teams may successfully stay in the Performing stage indefinitely if these changes — and their resulting behaviors — are recognized and handled directly.

Stage 5: Termination/Ending

Some teams do come to an end, when their work is completed or when the organization's needs change. While not part of Tuckman's original model, it is important for any team to pay attention to the end or termination process.

Feelings
Members of the team might experience a range of worries in light of the probable breakup of the group. They can be experiencing some worry as a result of ambiguity regarding their specific function or upcoming obligations. They can experience melancholy or a sense of loss as a result of the upcoming changes to their team dynamics. In addition, team members could

experience intense satisfaction with the group's successes. Individual members may experience all of these things at once or may alternate between feelings of loss and satisfaction. Individual and team morale may increase or decrease over the closing period due to these contradictory emotions. There is a good chance that team members will be feeling various emotions at any time regarding the team's ending.

Behaviors

Some team members may lose concentration on the team's tasks and become less productive during the Closing Stage. As an alternative, some team members may discover that concentrating on the current task helps them deal with their grief or sense of loss. The efficiency of their work may improve.

Team Tasks

The team must be aware of the oncoming shift and the many emotions that members may be experiencing as a result of the group's impending disintegration. The team should concentrate on these three tasks during this phase:

- Finalizing any deliverables and wrapping up any unfinished teamwork
- A review of the team's methodology and final product with a focus on finding "lessons learned" and relaying these to the sponsor for use by future teams
- Putting up a closing ceremony that recognizes everyone's contributions and the team's accomplishments and officially ends this particular team's existence.

QUALITIES OF A SUCCESSFUL TEAM

A high-performing company is built on strong teams, and the achievement and efficiency of the firm may be primarily attributed to effective teamwork. The workplace may experience issues including inadequate organization, missing deadlines, and conflict if employees do not get along and collaborate successfully. The entire team and the company frequently gain a lot from effective teamwork. An effective team can collaborate to foster ideation and creativity, attacking issues with original approaches. Team members may feel empowered to use original thinking when coming up with ideas. When they collaborate well, they can teach one another new techniques, approaches, and information.

Collaboration frequently increases productivity and helps to produce better business outcomes. Employees may become more motivated by participating in productive teams. They can acknowledge their efforts and bear some responsibility for the accomplishments of an organization. Whether working alone or as a member of a dysfunctional team, individuals may experience stress that successful teams can help alleviate.

Several businesses credit their employees' performance and team chemistry for their success. For all, poor teamwork frequently results in subpar output, which lowers the bottom line. Some managers make the incorrect assumption that assembling a team of capable, high-performing people is all it takes to achieve success. Successful teams, however, focused more on their interdependence than their membership.

What can teams do, then, to make sure that they are produced as a group and advance the company? Here are a few characteristics of a successful team.

1. Clear leadership

Effective leadership is a characteristic of successful teams, where one or more members take on the role of team captain. The whole team can then work together toward common objectives thanks to this. Successful leaders frequently offer direction, inspiration, and concentration. As the team faces a struggle, they could offer encouragement. A team may choose to routinely rotate its leadership, allowing each member to direct the group's activities. A sense of shared ownership and responsibility can be provided through shared leadership, thereby enhancing a team's performance.

2. Defined Goals

A successful team may first set its goals before beginning work on its tasks. The team may cooperate to determine shared goals that complement the organizational goals of a corporation. When project goals are important to team members, they may be more willing to dedicate themselves to achieving them. They can design strategies for achieving these objectives, delegating responsibilities, and establishing timetables.

Successful teams frequently decide how to assess their performance and the results of a project. This makes it easier for team members to grasp their goals and recognize when a task is finished. A group may routinely examine its objectives to see if any alterations are necessary.

3. Assigned Roles

When each team member has a clear understanding of their responsibilities, they may effectively contribute to the group and ensure its success. These responsibilities may be assigned by the team leader, or the group as a whole may decide how to best assess one another's abilities and knowledge to assign positions appropriately. Depending on its overarching objectives, the team could decide on specific responsibilities. When launching a marketing campaign as opposed to creating a new product, for instance, a team may have various roles.

When putting together a team, a leader may decide what positions are necessary. This enables them to identify team members who complement the assigned responsibilities the best. The duties of a team may vary as a project progresses. Once a leader has assembled the group, effective teams frequently reevaluate positions to make sure each member can meet the requirements of their roles.

4. Open Communication

Members of a team with open communication are more likely to discuss their thoughts and believe that their opinions count. Diverse perspectives are frequently welcomed by successful teams as they aid in problem-solving and task completion. Active listening is another component of effective communication, where team members consciously make an effort to hear their teammates' thoughts and pause before answering. It is necessary for monitoring development and collaborating effectively on projects. Crossed wires caused by inadequate communication may result in incomplete or erroneous work or conflicts. This enables a team to pool its knowledge, try out novel concepts, and collaborate to create successful plans.

5. Collaboration

To finish work and achieve team goals, effective teams rely on collaboration. When challenges develop, collaboration entails asking for assistance and exchanging ideas with one another. Team members may communicate often throughout a project to make sure they are focusing on the appropriate duties and helping to achieve the desired results. With the sharing of ideas and the combined knowledge of a team, collaborative work fosters innovation.

6. They Have Fun And Are Organized

There shouldn't be any work without some play! It's crucial to add some happiness to work life as this can cause burnout and a lack of productivity. Teams that get along exceptionally well enjoy one another's company and occasionally meet together outside of the workplace for socializing and fun! Developing good relationships with your coworkers can lead to a much more laid-back atmosphere and less tension.

For a firm to operate smoothly, the organization is crucial. Without it, the workplace may become chaotic, making it unlikely that goals will be met. Although each person should be in charge of managing their workload, management should make sure that everything is going according to schedule and that everyone on the team is finishing their task quickly. Making sure everyone is on the same page and deadlines are reached can be achieved by holding regular meetings.

<u>CHAPTER SUMMARY</u>

- A management strategy for improving workgroup performance and effectiveness is team development.

- Developing an effective team involves knowledge, research, and observation, with the organization's goals serving as inspiration.

- It is common practice to employ managers who have good team-building abilities. Establishing team rules and engaging in daily engagement can help teams grow naturally.

- Team members or an outside facilitator can lead structured exercises and activities.

- The talents and weaknesses of each team member must be noted, and managers must encourage participation, communication, and stress management.

- Active listening and varied viewpoints are welcomed in open communication, which also ensures accurate and conflict-free work.

- Teams may stay focused and in line with organizational goals with the support of well-defined goals and strategies, as well as frequent reviews.

- Collaboration encourages creativity, makes it possible to ask for assistance, and ensures that everyone is concentrating on the right tasks.

- Instead of focusing on membership, effective teams emphasize their interdependence.

- Clear leadership offers inspiration, focus, and direction, and shared leadership can improve performance.

CHAPTER TWO

MEANING OF TEAM LEADER

A team leader is someone who gives advice, direction, direction-setting, and leadership to a group of people (the team) to achieve a key result or set of related results. Team leaders act as the compass for a collection of people striving to achieve the same organizational goal. The team leader keeps track of the team's quantitative and qualitative successes and presents findings to management. As a team member, the leader frequently does the same tasks as other team members while also taking on additional "leader" responsibilities. This is in contrast to higher-level management, which frequently has a completely different job function. The team leader must inspire the group to "apply their knowledge and talents to achieve the common goals" for the group to work well. A team can work in a goal-oriented manner when the team leader inspires others. A "team leader" is someone who can motivate a group of people's performance. To build a successful team, team leaders draw on their experience, that of their colleagues, influence, and/or creativity.

When teams are aware of their mission, purpose, goals, and objectives, they can work effectively. It is the responsibility of the team leader to communicate this knowledge and set clear expectations for team members' roles, duties, and work standards. Group leaders must also communicate any updated or new corporate policies, procedures, or practices that may have an impact on the team's goals. Assuring that every team member knows what is necessary for productive work is the aim. Team leaders can discover difficulties or challenges inside the team and determine what needs to be resolved with the aid of this open channel of communication and information exchange.

Team leaders assist their members in overcoming obstacles that hinder production. They pinpoint problems that are impairing performance and direct the group toward overcoming obstacles with workable solutions. Group leaders address issues with suggested solutions to their managers if they fall outside of their purview. For instance, the team leader can start a one-on-one conversation with a team member if they are not contributing. If the issue persists, the team leader has the option of consulting his management or suggesting disciplinary action. A good team leader will always see a project through to completion and provide support and direction. Team leadership is about getting a lot of people to work together to achieve a goal, but this cannot happen effectively unless everyone understands their respective roles. Team members are given specific tasks by their leaders that are appropriate for their backgrounds and position. In addition to being in charge of the project's outcome, a leader is also in charge of assembling a capable team. Successful team leaders are aware of the quantity and kind of assistance each team member requires to carry out their responsibilities within a project.

A good team leader wouldn't, for instance, assign a novice employee to a project with significant responsibilities. Instead, he or she can assign the worker to a team member who excels at cooperating with others and comprehending the tasks at hand. A frequent tactic of effective leadership is to develop a strong team through well-considered working relationships.

QUALITIES OF A GOOD TEAM LEADER

Although it is a challenging job, team leadership is necessary for success. A skilled team leader can set clear objectives and expectations and is patient and empathetic. They motivate their team to be their best selves on and off the battlefield by setting an excellent example, being accessible when required, and doing so. When necessary, they give guidance and inspiration, but they also give freedom for innovation and development. A team member is more likely to follow a leader who possesses a diversity of features and qualities. Team leaders might develop their leadership abilities through formal education and practical experience, or they can be born with particular traits like compassion and honesty. The traits of a successful team leader inspire the team's respect and trust, which in turn boosts output at work.

Above all, a good team leader is patient because they are aware that success does not happen quickly. Take note of the traits stated below and concentrate on cultivating them in yourself if you want to manage a team in the future.

1. Ability To Communicate

The ability to effectively communicate is a must for team leaders. They must be able to communicate with their team effectively to ensure that everyone is aware of the team's objectives and is on the same page. They must also be able to communicate information clearly and swiftly when necessary so that the team can proceed as intended.

Giving timely feedback is another aspect of successful communication that enables team members to work better. To ensure that all team members are on board with their goals, leaders must also have a clear vision for the group and be able to communicate it effectively.

2. Keen Problem-Solving Skills

A competent team leader is someone who can think creatively, come up with novel solutions, inspire their team, and persuade them to cooperate as a group..They must also possess exceptional problem-solving abilities to recognize and address any concerns that may arise. This entails being able to approach an issue from various perspectives, generate potential solutions, and then choose which one is the most effective. It also calls for effective communication so that team members can stay informed and offer criticism as necessary.

Finally, to keep everyone on task, a competent team leader should be able to spot issues and rapidly resolve them.

3. Possessing A Positive Attitude

A good team leader can motivate his or her team and bring out the best in them. Effective communication, diplomatic dispute management, patience, a keen understanding of people, and attention to detail are all skills they must possess. These abilities are necessary to guide a productive team toward its goals. Keeping everyone motivated and concentrated on the task at hand requires being happy and pleasant. It might even motivate them to give it their all.

Positive attitude entails;

- Maintaining an optimistic attitude in the face of adversity
- Accepting criticism and modifying your strategy in response to team members' suggestions
- Leading by example – Setting the tone of the team, both physically and emotionally, and so on.

4. Understanding Group Dynamics

Everyone who wants to lead a team must possess the ability to comprehend group dynamics. It aids managers in better comprehending the team members they manage and how to best enlist their support for organizational objectives. To be effective, a team has to feel appreciated and motivated.

To ensure that everyone on the team develops as a member of the team, leaders must also promote open communication and feedback. Leaders that possess this information are better equipped to maximize the performance of their workforce and assist them in realizing their full potential.

Understanding group dynamics means;

- Knowing team member's personalities and strengths
- Dealing with conflict by building consensus, not enforcing one person's view at the expense of the others
- Supporting team members when they need it – sometimes being a shoulder to cry on or a sounding board
- Encouraging teamwork and creativity so that everyone can contribute their best ideas
- Keeping communication open – allowing team members to share their thoughts and feelings, both good and bad
- Having an understanding of group dynamics can help leaders create a positive team culture and inspire employees to do their best.

5. Vision And Strategic Thinking

For leaders, having a distinct vision and using strategic thinking is essential. Without one, team members may experience low morale and lose faith in the boss. Leaders must have good planning abilities as well as the flexibility to rapidly adjust when things don't go as planned to effectively carry out a vision. They may maintain the motivation and goal-focused ness of their team in this way. Team members also need to have faith that their leader has their best interests in mind, especially in the face of challenging circumstances or unforeseen setbacks. Team leaders need to set an example by acting honorably and being candid about communication problems. This will increase trust between them and the team as a whole.

6. Fairness And Good Judgment

Leaders need sound judgment and the ability to act quickly in complicated situations. Team members frequently defer to the leader because they have confidence in their judgment. While still being mindful of the distinctive talents and contributions of each team member, leaders must be fair and consistent in their expectations. Leaders should carefully analyze all the facts at their disposal before making challenging decisions. This enables them to produce a well-informed solution, satisfy the requirements of the team, and accomplish management's or the company's goals.

7.   Understanding   Emerging Technologies

Team leaders must have a solid understanding of the latest technology as the globe transitions to a more digital future. They must be able to stay up with the always-evolving trends and have a solid grasp of how technology functions.

They will be more equipped to implement new technology into their team's operations and create creative plans as a result.

Team leaders can acquire the knowledge and skills necessary for leading a technologically savvy team by taking initiative and being supportive of employee training. To decide how to employ new technology most effectively, leaders must also be aware of the hazards that could arise from their use.

Also, to avoid impeding productivity or innovation across the entire organization, leadership must be proactive in anticipating needs and ensuring that everyone's skill sets are kept up to date.

Conclusion

You must comprehend what makes a good team leader in your capacity as the team leader. You may create a supportive and effective work environment by realizing the value of team leadership.

Also, many leadership philosophies might work in certain situations. Learn more about the various traits of a strong team leader and how to cultivate them within yourself. Start assembling a productive and cohesive team right away

STRATEGIES TO DEVELOP YOUR TEAM

You may be the finest in your field. Yet, if you don't know how to assemble an outstanding team around you, that won't matter in the long run. Your startup might offer exactly what the community needs, but if your team members can't get along, it won't succeed. Even though you might be overjoyed to get promoted to team leader at work, if you can't establish trust with the people you supervise, your team won't be successful.

That old saying, "Teamwork makes the dream work," is always going to be true. A group of people in sync can build something great from the ground up. Together, you can take advantage of each other's strengths to do what you never could alone. Putting people together might seem simple, but building a truly effective team requires talent. If you're wondering how to form a team, keep in mind that every successful group effort begins with a talented, driven leader.

That kind of leader understands how to maximize the abilities of each team member so that you can jointly achieve your most ambitious objectives. You've come to the perfect place if you want to learn how to lead effectively and assemble a dream team. Although there is a process involved, we'll walk you through nine alternative approaches to assembling your squad.

The Importance Of Teamwork!;
The underrated force behind every great company is teamwork. A business might not reach its full potential without a well-managed crew. Each member of your team has the potential to contribute their special talents and skills, but for that to happen, teamwork is necessary.

In one study, 50% of the firms polled claimed that employee collaboration aided them in achieving their operational objectives. That indicates that the other 50% still had difficulty achieving their objectives, demonstrating the value of having a productive team.

You won't benefit from grouping your personnel if they don't have defined objectives. They also need to have clear goals and assigned roles for each member. It may be a huge triumph for your company when your staff is in sync. It has been found that workers who cooperate frequently at work are more motivated, achieve their goals, and feel less worn out.

Because they will feel more connected to one another, teamwork also has the potential to enhance the well-being of your staff. And your company will undoubtedly expand as a result when your staff is content and productive.

Employees who work well together consider the overall goal they hope to accomplish. They will decide to cooperate rather than compete to achieve that aim. Departmental and smaller team silos can be broken down through teamwork. Everyone in the organization will be able to perform their tasks more effectively by better understanding one another.

Third, collaboration is crucial since it provides excellent learning opportunities. By working together with more seasoned personnel, less experienced employees can learn. Senior team members may get the chance to hone their leadership abilities and discover how to form productive teams. In the end, this will give everyone the chance to advance their careers, which is a terrific approach to increasing employee satisfaction.

Ready to learn how to build your team?
Start by following these strategies to create a strong and successful team:

1. Establish Company Culture.

The corporate culture should be established from the start so that a new team is aware of what is expected of them. This will demonstrate proper conduct and work methodology to your team. Also, remember your responsibility as a leader. The best way to make sure that everyone continues on the correct path is to be an effective facilitator of these team principles.

2. Define everyone's roles and responsibilities.

Everyone needs to be aware of their particular responsibilities if they want to understand how to create a successful team. Although teamwork is collaborative, efficient operations also call for solo work. Make sure your team members understand their roles and responsibilities. You should make sure they understand exactly what they are expected to do.

The individuals you are managing should also be aware of who to contact in the event of a team conflict or inquiries regarding their job.

3. Ensure That Everyone Feels Respected.

Team members should feel respected on all levels, as both workers and people. They are not machines. The inner selves, emotions, and personality traits of your team members define who they are in reality. Seeing your employees as a whole demonstrates respect for them. Their self-esteem and well-being will increase as a result. It may even lead to an increase in productivity, which is great for the company.

4. Stay As Organized As You Can.

Organized leaders are effective. They closely monitor team dynamics and frequently inquire about employee well-being. Set up project management methods and organizational procedures as soon as you begin learning how to create a powerful team. This will prevent you from becoming overburdened and promote the success of your team.

5. Motivate with positivity.

Also, great leaders believe that "you get more flies with honey than vinegar." In the actual world, this means that shaping behavior using positive rewards as opposed to negative reinforcement is more effective. Avoid the temptation to point out the errors of your teammates. Instead, foster a good team climate by highlighting instances and actions that you found particularly commendable and encouraging your team to continue in that vein. Shaming people who made mistakes is a much less effective strategy for encouraging team performance.

6. Communicate As Much As You Can.

We all enjoy knowing where we stand as humans. Are my coworkers satisfied with the work I'm producing? Do I have anything to work on? Assume that everyone is curious. Your performance will suffer if they can see you're unhappy but don't say anything about it. This can cause stress to build up and even animosity. They may have an unpleasant shock when you inform them that they have been underperforming if they believe they are doing a wonderful job but you, their supervisor, aren't happy with their performance. Therefore brush up on your communication abilities because poor communication can swiftly destroy business connections while great communication can keep them strong for decades.

7. Look For Ways To Reward Good Work.

Individuals enjoy having their efforts validated. This is a fantastic approach to express gratitude if you're in a position to do so financially. Consider alternative ways to express appreciation and trust if you are a company with limited resources. A simple method is to practice delegation. Let a team member who demonstrates sound judgment take on certain important decisions that you may have previously saved for yourself. Permit them to use the business credit card if they have a reputation for being especially frugal with money.

Pick a little approach to demonstrate that you value your employees' efforts and are paying close attention to them. It will enhance your reputation as a manager and serve to remind staff members that they are important team members.

8. Be Open To Giving And Receiving Feedback

Without going over our errors, we cannot improve. However, even when nothing is wrong, team members can benefit from constructive criticism and thorough feedback.

It can also proactively avoid problems. Be an excellent listener when it comes time for you to get input on a problem. Leaders and team members will be better able to handle issues in the future when they can use feedback to their benefit. That's one of the best approaches to discovering how to create a long-lasting team that works well together.

9. Celebrate People's Wins.

This collaborative effort merits recognition. Keep an eye out for outstanding teamwork, and don't be afraid to praise it. Certain objectives could be impossible for a single person to accomplish but simple for a group. Honoring your team's efforts fosters a culture where employees are motivated to take chances and achieve more. Even if they fail, they will be confident in their support system.

10. Value Your Team's Diversity.

Dealing with individuals that have various viewpoints and experiences will only be beneficial to your company. You should value the qualities that make your personnel distinctive rather than downplay them. Members of the team will benefit from feeling secure enough to be themselves as a result.

As a team leader, try your best to be adaptable and accessible.

CHAPTER SUMMARY

- A team leader provides guidance, leadership, and advice to a group of individuals to accomplish a set of connected goals.

- They keep tabs on the team's accomplishments, both quantitative and qualitative, and report them to management. Team leaders encourage and inspire their colleagues to accomplish shared objectives.

- Because it creates learning opportunities, dismantles silos, and raises employee happiness, collaboration is essential.

- Establishing business culture, clearly defining duties and responsibilities, ensuring that everyone feels valued, being organized, inspiring with positivity, and communicating as much as possible are all essential for creating a successful team.

- To stay motivated and goal-focused, vision and strategic thinking are essential, and making informed decisions requires fairness and excellent judgment.

- Leading a technologically savvy team requires an understanding of emerging technology, which includes keeping up with trends, encouraging staff training, and being proactive to avoid stifling productivity or innovation.

- For any organization to succeed and realize its full potential, building a strong and successful team is crucial.

www.ingramcontent.com/pod-product-compliance
Lightning Source LLC
Chambersburg PA
CBHW071144220526
45467CB00015B/1833